What Color were Prehistoric Sharks and Rays?

A Prehistoric Times Coloring book

By Mike Fredericks, and Tracy Lee Ford

ISBN-13: 978-1983692390

ISBN-10: 1983692395

This book is dedicated to the great fish/fossil fish artist extraordinaire, Ray Troll, because some of these interpretations of fossil sharks would not be possible, except for his work.

Genus pronunciation chart; (editor's note, some of these are the best 'guess', and etymologies that I could find, and they may be incorrect. T. Ford).

AelloposIschyodus, Greek, Aello/Aellopos, Harpy sister, & *Ischyodus,* Aell·oh·pos·Is·chy·oh·dus

Belantsea, (named after a legendary ancestor of the Crow Nation), be·lant·see·ah

Brandringa, named in honor of Mr. Ray Brandringa, Brand·ring·ah·ray·eye

Carcharias, Greek, karkharías, 'shark', car·char·eye·as,

Carcharocles, Greek, Karchos, 'sharpen', Greek, kleos, 'glory, fame', car·char·oh·kleh·es

Carcarhodon, Greek, Karchos, 'sharpen', Greek, odus, 'teeth', car·char·oh·don

Chlamydoselachus, Greek, chlamys, -idos, 'cloak, cape' Greek, selachos, 'shark', Cla·mid·oh·se·lach·us.

Chondrenchelys, Greek, chondr- 'cartilage', Latin, ren, 'kidney', Latin, Chelys, 'tortoise', Chond·ren·chel·ys

Cladoselache, Latin, clad, 'slaughter', Greek, selachos, 'shark'. clad·o·sel·a·che

Cobelodus, Greek, cobele, 'a needle', Greek, odus, 'tooth', co·bel·oh·dus

Cretoxyrhina, creto- for "Cretaceous, Oxyrhina, 'sharp-nosed', Creto·oxy·rhin·ah

Cyclobatis, Greek, Kuklos, 'circle', Greek, batis, 'ray', Cy·clo·bat·is

Diablodontus, Diablo, devil, Greek, odon, 'tooth'; Die·abe·lo·oh·don·tus.

Echinochimaera, Greek, echinos, 'spiny', & Chimaera, e·chin·oh·chi·mare·ah

Edestus, Greek, edeste, 'devour', e·des·tes

Eonotidanus, Greek, eos, 'dawn', Greek, notos, 'back', Greek, danos, 'dry, shriveled'; eo·noto·ti·dan·us.

Falcatus, Latin, falcatus, 'sickle-shaped', Fawl·cat·us

Goodrichthyes, In honor of Goodrich? Greek, ichthys 'fish', dood·rich·thyes

Harpacanthus Greek, Harpagos, 'grappling hooks', Greek, akantha, 'thorn' Har·pa·gos·ak·an·thah·us

Helicoprion, Greek, Helix 'spiral', Greek, prioni, 'saw'. hel·ah·co·pri·on

Heliobatus, Greek, helios, 'sun', Greek, batis, 'ray', he·li·os·bat·is

Heterodontus, Greek, heteros, 'different', Greek, odon, 'tooth', het·ero·don·tus

Holomacanthus, Greek, holom, 'the whole', Greek, akanthos, 'spine, thorn', hol·om· ak·an·thah·us

Hybodus, Greek, hybo, 'hump', Greek, odon, 'tooth', hy·boh·dus

Iniopteryx, Greek, inion, 'nape', Greek, pteryx, 'fin', in·ion·pter·yx,

Isthyodus, Greek, ichthys, 'strength', Greek, odon, 'tooth', is·chy·oh·dus

Janassa, named after someone? Ja·nass·ah

Leptostyrax, Greek, leptos, 'thin, fine, slender', Greek, styrax, 'spike at the end of a spear but' lept·oh·sty·rax

Libanopristis, in references to the country Libanon, Greek, pristis, 'sawfish', Iib·an·on·pris·tis

Lonchidon, Greek, lonche, 'spear', Greek, odon, 'tooth', lon·chie·oh·don

Menaspis, In reference to the people of Mena'pii?, Greek, aspis, 'shield', men·ah·as·pis

Mobula, etymology of *Mobula* is unknown, Mob·u·la

Myledaphus, Greek, myle, 'grinder', Greek, edaphos, 'bottom', my·lee·e·daph·us

Onchipristis, Greek, Oncho, 'Large', Greek, pristis, 'sawfish', ON-koh-PRIST-tis

Orectolobus Greek, oryktos, 'to digger', Greek, lobos, 'lobe', oh·rick·tos·low·boos

Ornithoprion, Greek, ornithos, 'bird', Greek, prion, 'saw', or·nith·oh·pri·on

Orthacanthus, Greek, orthos, 'straight', Greek, akanthos, 'spine, thorn', or·tho·ak·an·thah·us

Otodus, Greek, ous, 'ear', Greek, odus, 'tooth', OH·toe·dus

Palaeoscyllium, Greek, palaeo, 'ancient', Latinized Greek, scyllium (skylion), meaning dogfish, pa·leo·sci·llee·um

Phorcynis, Greek, Phoro, 'bearer, to bear', Greek, cynis? fore·cye·nis

Polysentor, Greek, poly, 'many', and? In reference to the many sensory lines on the spines, poly·sen·tor

Pristiophorus, Greek, pristis, 'sawfish', Greek, oph, 'eye', & orus, Egyptian god? PRIST·tis·oph·or·us

Promexyele, Greek, promeces, 'elongated', Greek, xyele, 'rasp', pro·me·xy·el·ee,

Protospinax, Greek, proto, 'first, Latin, spina, 'spine', pro·to·spine·ax

Pseudomegachasma, Greek, pseudes, 'false', plus Megachasma, sue·doh·mega·chas·ma

Ptychodus, Greek, ptychos 'folding', Greek, odon, 'tooth', ti·cho·dus

Rajorhina, Latin, raia, 'ray', Greek, rhinae, a type of shark whose skin arrows are made; Rah·jo·rhin·ah

Romerodus, named in honor of the paleontologist Alfred Romer, Greek, odon, 'tooth', Row·mer·oh·dus

Sarcoprion, Greek, sarx, 'flesh', Greek, prion, 'saw', Sar·co·pri·on

Scapanorhynchus Greek, skapanē, 'spade', New Latin o + rhynchus, 'snout'; Ska·pane·oh·rhyn·chus

Sibyrhynchus, Sibyne, a hunting spear, Greek, rhynchos, 'snout', si·by·rhin·chos

Sphenacanthus, Greek, sphen, 'a wasp, Greek, akantha, 'thorn', Sphen·ak·an·thah·

Sphyra, Greek, sphyra 'hammer', Sfi·rha

Squalicorax, Latin, Squalus, 'shark', Greek, Korax, 'raven', Squal·eye·kor·ax

Stethacanthus, Greek stēthos, 'chest', Greek, akanthos, 'spine, thorn', ste·thos·ak·an·thah·us

Triodus, Greek, tri-, 'three', and Greek, odus, 'tooth', tri·oh·dus

Tristychius, Greek, treis, 'three', Greek, stichos, 'a row', tri·stick·us

Xenacanthus, Greek, xenos, 'strange', Greek, akantha, 'thorn', Xen·ak·an·thah·us.

Wodnika, named after a person? wod·nik·ah

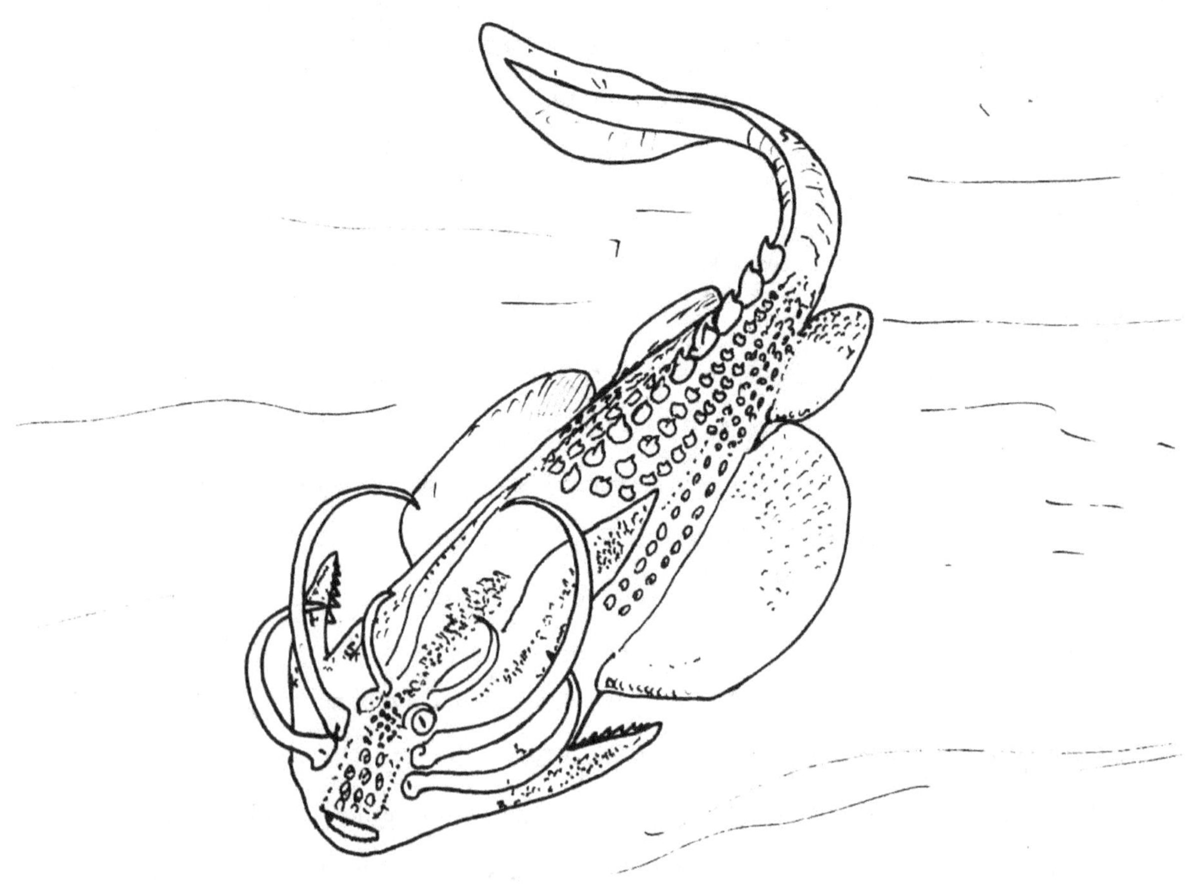

Menaspis armata was named by Ewald, in 1848. It is only known from one, fairly complete specimen. It is a strange looking holocephalian, i.e. Chimaerian. It has three pairs of long spines on its head, dorsally placed eyes, and supraorbital sensory canal that runs in the skin, hat is surrounded by modified denticles, which are modified teeth that forms the scales on the body of the shark. It lived in the oceans of Germany, during the Late Permian. It was small, less than 15 centimeters long.

Helicoprion was a long-lived, most bizarre appearing genus of extinct shark. Almost all fossil specimens are comprised of spirally arranged clusters of the individuals' teeth, called "tooth whorls" which were strongly reminiscent of a circular saw. For over a century, where the tooth-whorl was in the lower jaw was uncertain, but many possibilities were theorized, as well as its anatomy and behavior. More recently, Brad Matsen and artist Ray Troll proposed that no teeth were present in the animal's top jaw besides the crushing teeth for the whorl to cut against. *Helicoprion* lived in the oceans of the early Permian 290 million years ago, with species known from North America, Eastern Europe, Asia, and Australia. It is believed it used its unique teeth to crush the shells of sea creatures. One tooth whorl from a *Helicoprion* discovered in Idaho measured 18 inches in length meaning the shark would have been over thirty feet in length, and another, even bigger tooth whorl that was discovered was 24" long and would have belonged to an animal that possibly exceeded 39 ft in length, making *Helicoprion* a very large shark.

During the Solnhofen (Late Jurassic) Germany was dotted with small islands. The ocean was warm like modern tropical areas. Marine, terrestrial and flying animals, both invertebrates and vertebrates, were extremely abundant. Here a Woebegone shark, *Orectolobus jurassicus,* is feeding on a primitive shark, *Palaeoscyllium formosum,* while a cuttlefish, *Leptoteuthis gigas,* swims above the sharks, with a horseshoe crab, *Mesolimulus walchi* and the small shrimp *Aeger* sp are walking nearby.

Cladoselache lived in the Devonian period. This primitive shark grew to about six feet long and hunted the oceans of North America. *Cladoselache* is one of the best known of the early sharks in part due to the well-preserved fossils that were discovered in the Cleveland Shale on the south shore of Lake Erie. In addition to the skeleton, the fossils were so well preserved that they included traces of skin, muscle fibers, and internal organs, such as the kidneys. It had from five to seven gill slits, and a short, rounded snout that had a mouth opening at the front of the skull. Its teeth were smooth-edged, making them suitable for grasping, but not tearing or chewing. Cladoselache also had a blade-like structure which was positioned in front of the dorsal fins. These anatomical features made swimming easier and faster. Cladoselache was almost entirely devoid of scales with the exception of small cusped scales on the edges of the fins, mouth and around the eyes. This helped with its speed and agility which was useful when trying to outswim its probable predator, the heavily armored 20-foot-long placoderm fish *Dunkleosteus*. Members of the *Cladoselache* genus were predatory sharks, and the well-preserved fossils found in the Cleveland Shale revealed a significant amount regarding their eating habits including their stomach contents. These remains included mostly small ray-finned bony fishes, shrimp-like fish and hagfish-like proto-vertebrates. Some of the fish remains were found tail first within the stomach, indicating that *Cladoselache* was a fast and agile hunter.

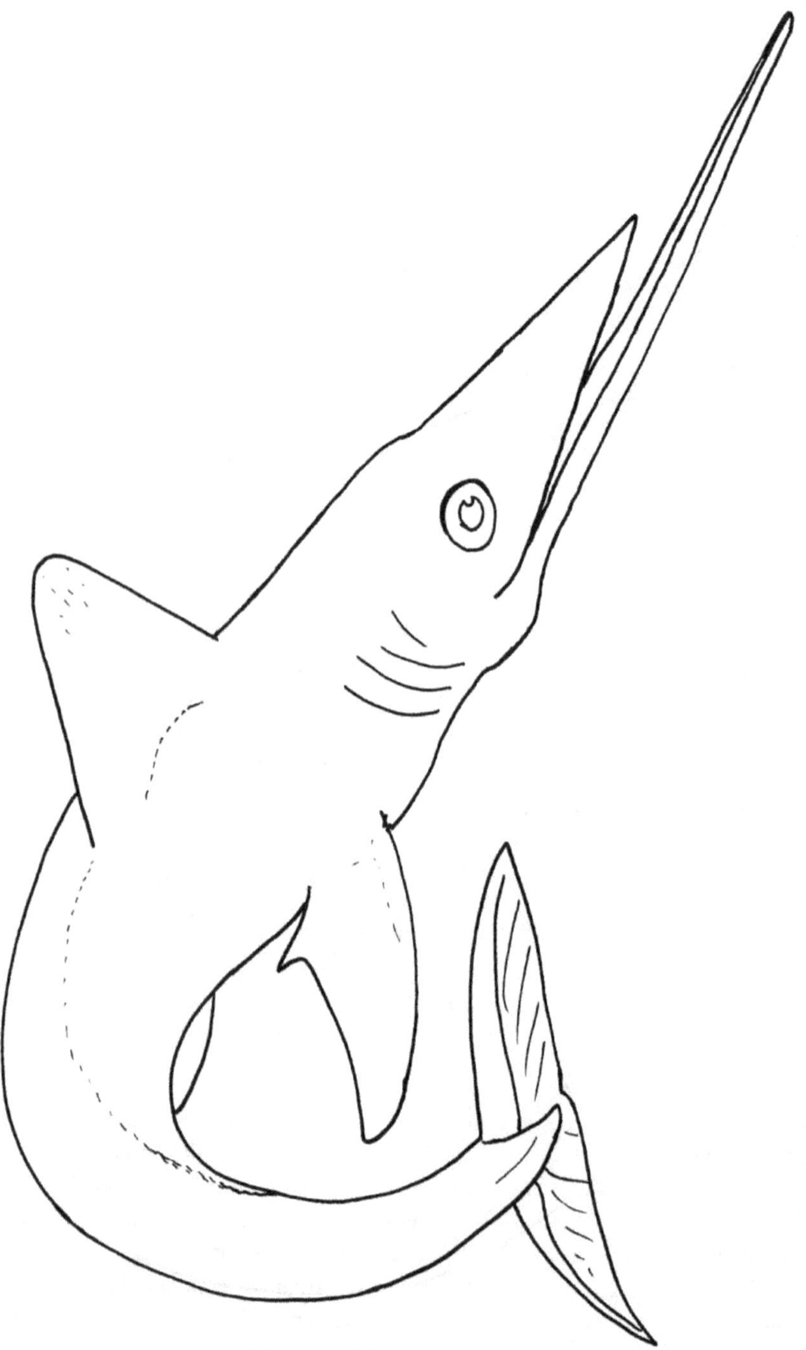

Ornithoprion hertwigi is an unusual early chondrichthian mainly from the late Pennsylvania (Upper Carboniferous) from Indiana. It is a Caseodontid, family Caseodontidae, primitive shark. The snout of this shark is pointed, and it has a very long, narrow, pointed lower jaw, which are sheathed with boney rods that formed the base of dermal denticles arranged in longitudinal rows. It was about half a meter long and lived in freshwater.

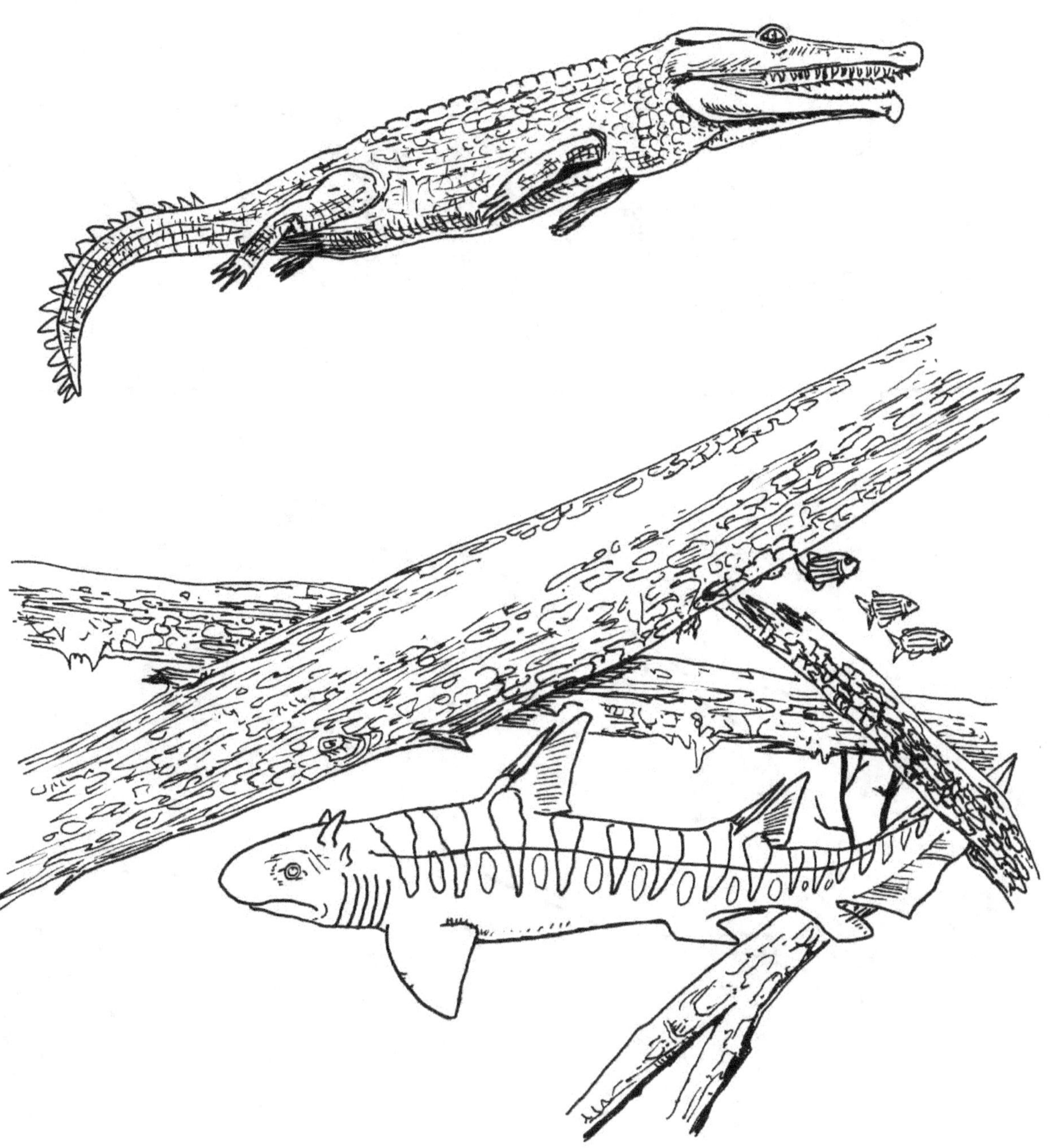

The prehistoric shark that looked like the Devil was a shark with horns and sharp teeth that survived Earth's biggest extinction. Devil Tooth or *Diablodontus michaeledmundi* was discovered in the Kaibab Formation of Flagstone, Arizona. Scientists at Northern Arizona University believe the 3.5 foot shark survived the Permian Triassic Extinction which wiped out 96% of life on Earth. The creature lived 260 million years ago and was a hump-toothed shark with a distinctive asymmetric fin similar to modern sharks. The hump-toothed shark terrorized the seas for around 50 million years but even the devil shark hid when large predators came close.

Myledaphus bipartitus is an abundant freshwater guitarfish. Numerous teeth have been found in North America during the Late Cretaceous. It was originally believed to have been some kind of freshwater sting ray. It wasn't until a nearly complete specimen from Dinosaur Provincial Park, Dinosaur Park Formation, Late Campanian, finally showed it to be a guitarfish. *Myledaphus* shows that both sting rays and guitarfish lived in freshwater lakes, streams, and rivers. Here a *Myledaphus* is feeding on a salamander, and in the background a heard of *Centrosaurus* begin crossing the river.

Onchopristis was a genus of extinct giant sawfish that lived in the Cretaceous in North Africa and New Zealand. It had an elongated snout lined laterally with barbed teeth. As with modern sawfish, *Onchopristis's* eyes were on top of its head, to spot predators rather than prey, and its mouth and gills were under its body. The rostrum, or snout, was around eight feet long, lined with barbed teeth. The rostrum most likely would have had electroreceptors to detect food in the water below them like most modern sharks and some rays. *Onchopristis* may have raked through the riverbed to find and then eat prey.

Romerodus orodontus is another Caseodontid shark. It was named after Alfred Sherwood Romer, one of the iconic paleontologist of the 20[th]century. It is a relatively small shark, not exceeding 50 centimeters in overall length. Nine partial or nearly complete specimens were found in the Stark Shales Dennis Formation, Late Carboniferous and Stark and Wea Shales of Papillion, LaPlatte, Nebraska. It has a small single dorsal fin, and two sets of very small pectoral fins.

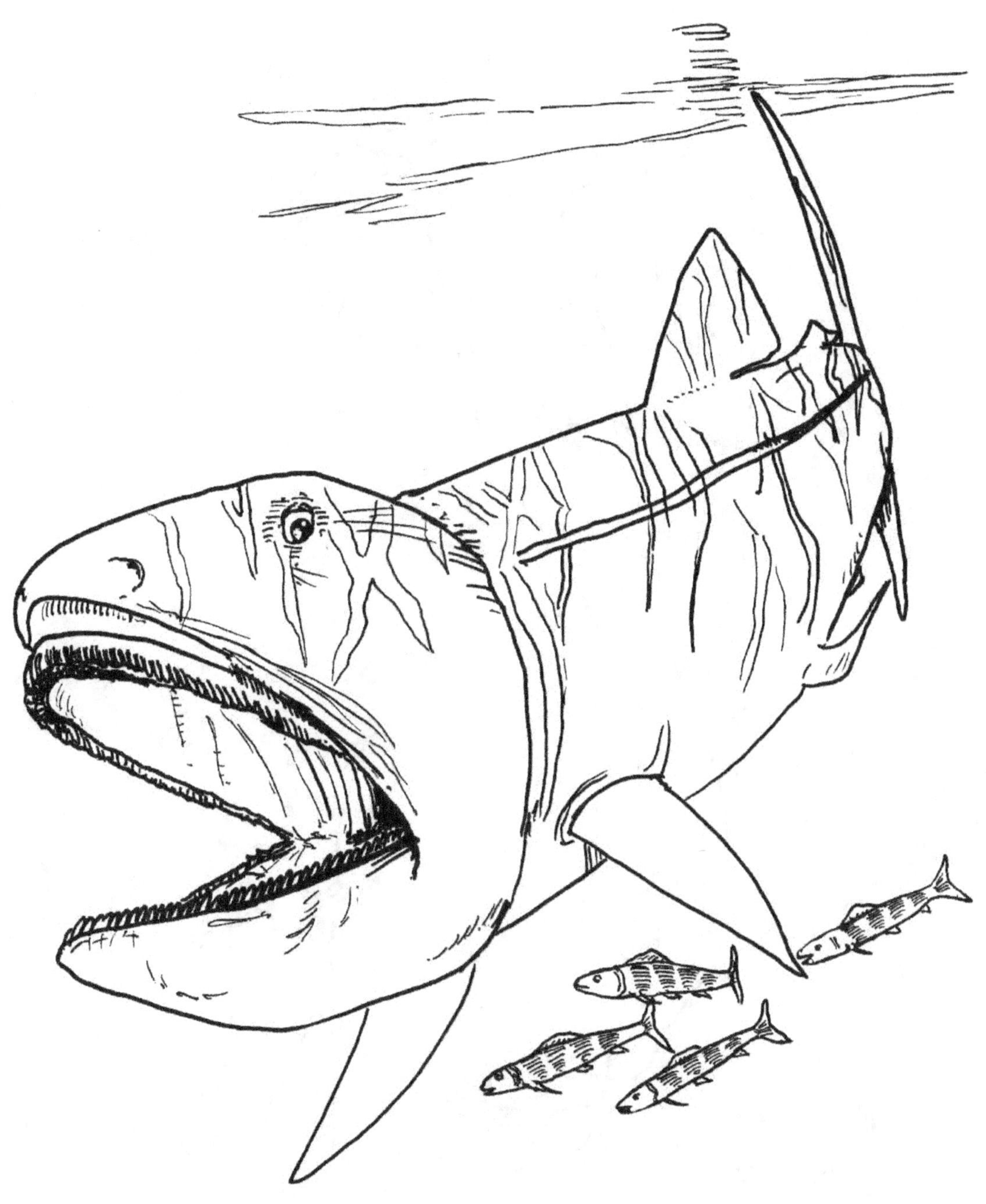

Pseudomegachasma ("false megamouth") is an extinct genus of filter-feeding shark that was closely related to the modern sand tiger shark. It swam the seas with its mouth open collecting plankton to eat. It is known from Cretaceous strata in Russia and the United States, and is the only known and oldest known planktivorous. It most likely derived from its closest relative, the piscivorous shark *Johnlongia*. As its name suggests, it was originally classified under *Megachasma*, before it was found to be an odontaspid.

Bandringa rayi, was named by Zangerl, 1969, in honor of Mr. Ray Brandringa, who first collected this strange looking shark. There were two species in the genus, *B. rayi*, and *B. herdinae*, which are now believed to be one genus. He found it in Mazon Creek, Illinois, which is a world famous fresh, to brackish water formation. What is unique about this small shark is its long rostrum. It was a bottom feeding shark. New research has shown that it migrated from the freshwater rivers, to the estuarine Mazon Creek waters which served as a nursery, which also served as a nursery for several different chondrichthyians. Here a *Bandringa* is chasing an early amphibian, *Amphibamus grandiceps*.

Scapanorhynchus ("Spade Snout") is an extinct genus of shark that lived from the early Cretaceous until possibly the Miocene. Their extreme similarities to the living goblin shark, *Mitsukurina owstoni*, lead some experts to consider reclassifying it as *Scapanorhynchus owstoni*. However, most shark specialists regard the goblin shark to be distinct enough from its prehistoric relatives to merit placement in its own genus. *Scapanorhynchus* had an elongated, albeit flattened snout and sharp awl-shaped teeth ideal for seizing fish, or tearing chunks of flesh from its prey. It was a small shark normally measuring about 65 centimeters, though the largest species, *S. texanus*, is thought to have reached up to 10 feet in length, about the size of a modern goblin shark. Here two face off with a plesiosaur.

Janassa bituminosa is an ancient chondrichthyian from the order Petalodontida. It had a pointed snout and a flattened body like a skate. Its mouth was on the underside of the body, like a ray's, with revolving flattened teeth in overlapping rows. It mainly fed on shellfish, mussels, brachiopods or sea lilies. It was about a meter long and 25 centimeters wide. It lived in the Lower Carboniferous to the Lower Permian, North America, Britain, Germany, Greenland, Czech Republic and Russia.

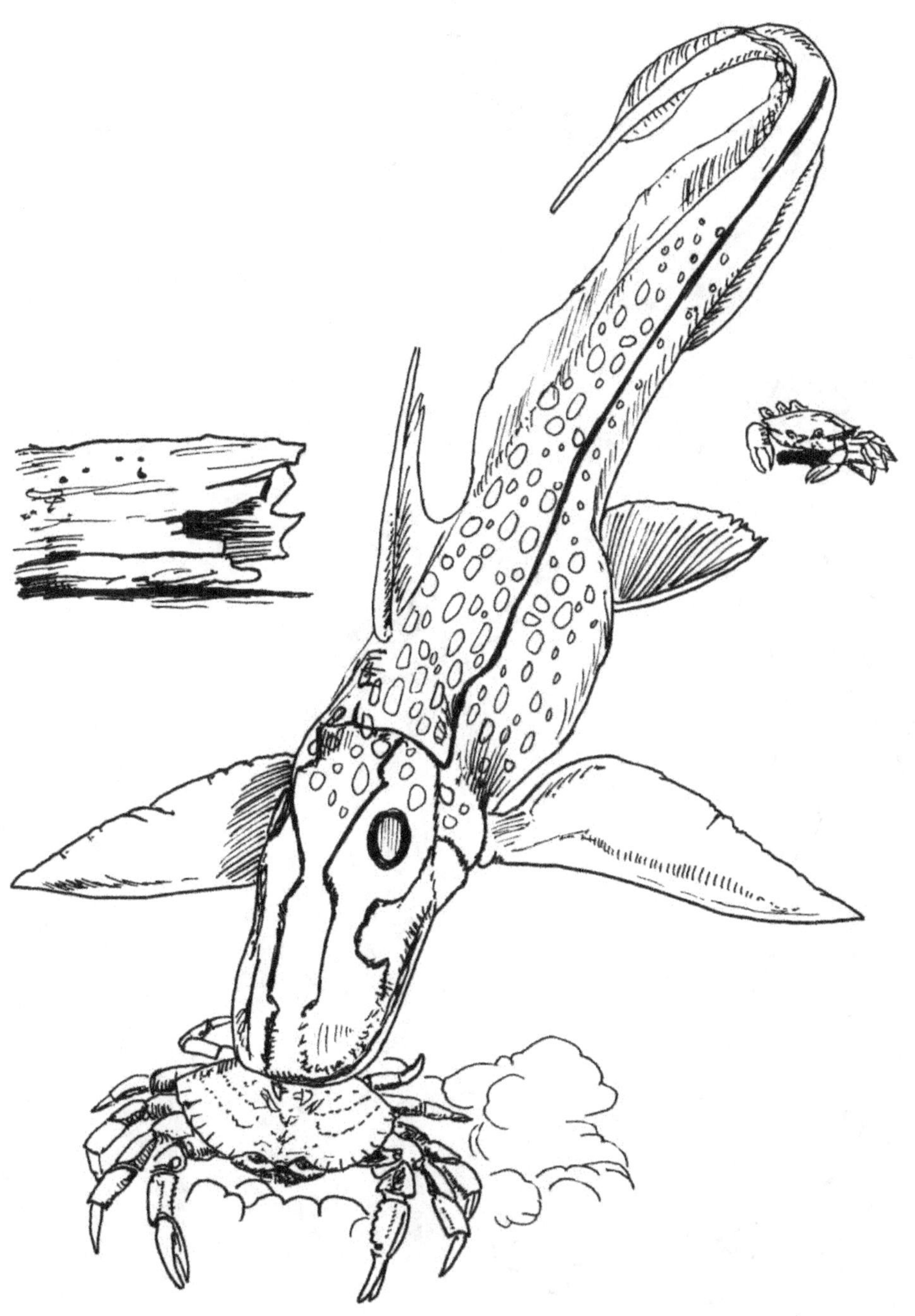

Ischyodus is an extinct genus of cartilaginous fish belonging to the subclass Holocephali, which includes the modern-day chimaeras. Fossils are known from Europe (including Russia), North America, and New Zealand. *Ischyodus* was rather similar to the present-day *Chimaera monstrosa*, which is found in the Atlantic Ocean and Mediterranean Sea. Just like *C. monstrosa*, _Ischyodus_ had large eyes, a long whip-like tail, small lips, large pectoral fins and dorsal fin, and a dorsal spike attached to the front of the dorsal fin. The spike probably served as a method of protection against predators, and may have been venomous, as it is in modern chimaeras. Dental plates of at least two species, *Ischyodus rayhaasi* and *Ischyodus dolloi*, have been found at several sites in North Dakota.

Sawsharks superficially look like Sawfish (which are rays), and are true sharks. The bill consists of numerus 'teeth', and like its relative Sawfish, was a bottom dwelling shark. The genus *Pristiophorus* goes back to the Late Santonian of Lebanon, Late Cretaceous, and has several living species today. *Pristiophorus tumidens* comes from the marine deposits of Sahel Alma, Lebanon, with a preserved length (lacking most of its tail) 50 centimeters in length.

Hybodus ("humped tooth") first appeared towards the end of the Permian period, and disappeared during the Late Cretaceous. The hybodont sharks were especially successful and could be found in shallow seas across the world. Hybodus species grew to almost seven feet in length, and are believed to have been opportunist predators. Although not very big, it had the classic streamlined shark shape, complete with two dorsal fins that would have helped it steer with precision. The mouth was not large, and rather than ruthlessly hunt large prey, *Hybodus*, was capable of eating a wide range of foods. They had several distinct features that made them stand apart from other primitive sharks. Firstly, they had two different types of teeth, suggesting a wide diet. The sharper teeth would have been used to catch slippery prey, while the flatter teeth probably helped them crush shelled creatures. Secondly, they had a bony blade on their dorsal fin that probably served a defensive function. The first fossilized teeth from *Hybodus* were found in England around 1845. Since then teeth (and dorsal spines) have been recovered from around the world.

Triodus sessilis has also been called *Xenacanthus sessilis*. It turns out that both *Triodus* and *Xenacanthus* are valid genera in the family Xenacanthidae. This family is a family of long bodied, long dorsal finned freshwater sharks. *Triodus* was one of the smaller genera, about a half meter long, *Xenacanthus* was a meter long and the largest xenacanthid is *Orthacantus senckenbergianus*, which was over three meters long. *Triodus* were a stalk-and-ambush hunters, and lived in the Early Permian of Germany. Here a *Triodus sessilis* is chasing several *Apateon amphibians*, with a freshwater coelacanthid, *Coelacanthus granulatus*.

About 260 million years ago, *Orthacanthus* was the apex predator of freshwater swamps and bayous in Europe and North America. Its body reached nearly 10 feet in length and the shark possessed a peculiar set of double-fanged teeth. These prehistoric sharks known as xenacanths had a long spine growing from the back of their skull and a very long dorsal fin, which ran all along its back giving it an eel-like appearance. They first appeared about 400 million years ago in the Devonian, and became extinct just before the Mesozoic, about 225 million years ago. *Orthacanthus* was likely cannibalistic, as teeth from juvenile *Orthacanthus* were found within the coprolites of adults. Here, an *Orthacanthus* is being chased by an *Eryops,* and is chasing a *Diplocaulus.*

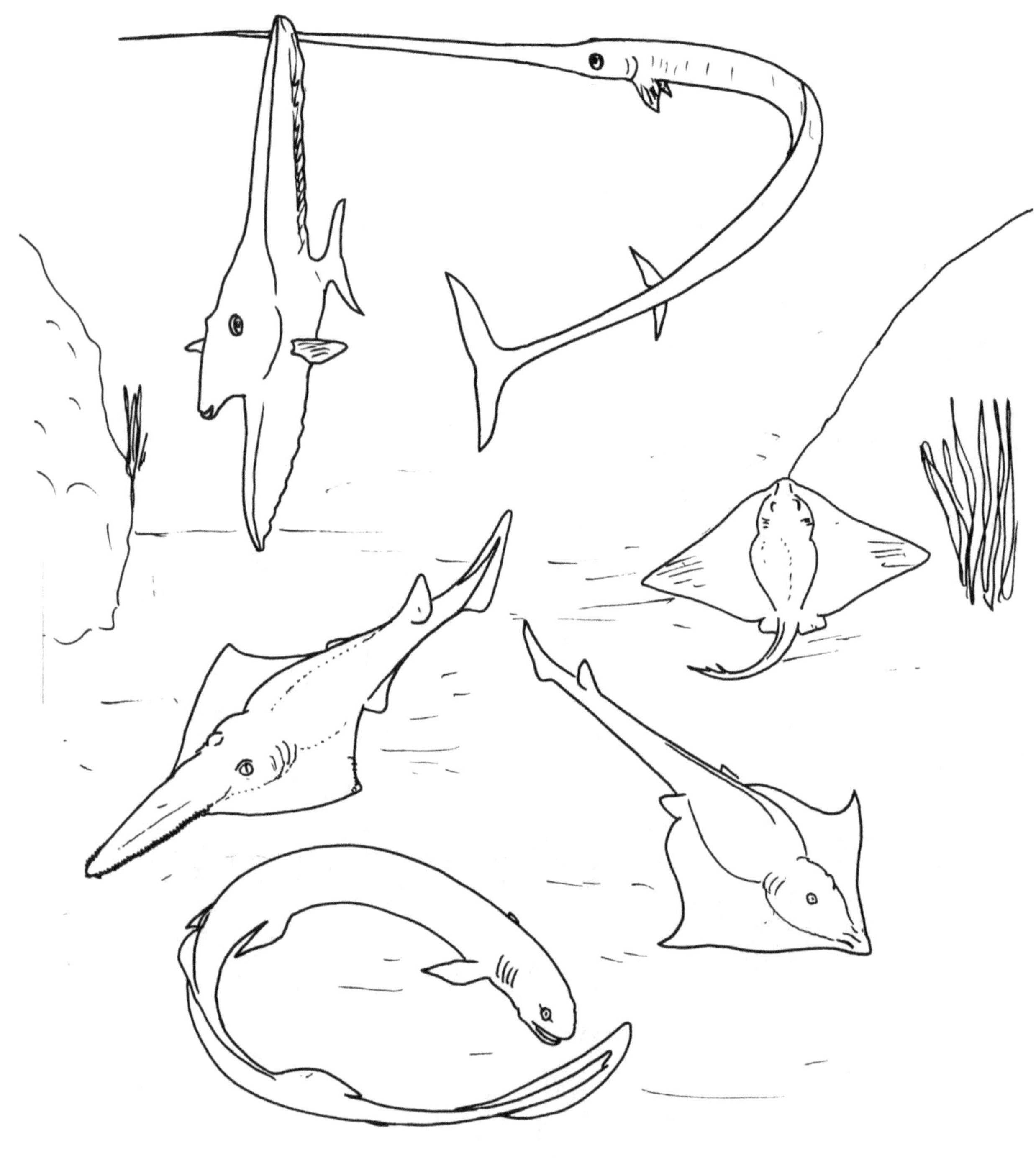

During the Cenomanian (middle Cretaceous) Lebanon was a shallow sea/near shore environment. Numerous fossil fish, and other vertebrate fossils have been found in shale in the area. Here are four different chondirchthyians and two fish. The chondrichthyians are; Lower left side is the long *Mesiata*, the middle left is the sawfish *Libanopristis hiram*; upper right is the ray *Rajorhina expansa*, and the lower ray is *Rajorhina sp*; The upper left fish is *Gebrayelichthys vexillarius* and the upper left is *Belonostomus* sp.

Belantsea (named after a legendary ancestor of the Crow Nation) is a genus of extinct petalodontid cartilaginous fish that lived during the Lower Carboniferous, about 350 million years ago. Its beautiful fossils are found in Bear Gulch Limestone. Its body was leaf-shaped, with muscular fins and a small tail. Such a body plan would allow for great maneuverability, but at the cost of speedy cruising. Its few, large, triangular teeth formed a beak-like arrangement that allowed it to graze bryozoans, sponges, crinoids, and other encrusting animals. The genus contains two species, *B. montana* and *B. occidentalis*. It appears to have been a proto-shark design. Below it, an *Echinochimaera*, an extinct genus of fish, is scared up from the sandy bottom. This ancient fish was assigned to the order chimaera. The two known *Echinochimaera* species lived in the Upper Mississippian. Fossils of the species were found in the Bear Gulch Limestone in Montana, United States. Both species have rounded bodies and paddle-like tails as well as large pectoral fins, two dorsal fins and a jaw fused to the braincase. The females only grew to about half the size of the males. Males also had four pairs of spikes which may have been used to defend against predators and to identify the fish as male.

Hammerhead sharks are an iconic shark. They live in warm tropical and temperate waters around the world. They first appeared in the Eocene, *Sphyrna latidens*, Order Carcharhiniformes, Family Sphyrnidae. The chondrychtians depicted here are from the Round Mountain Hill Formation (Shark Tooth Hill, Southern California), Middle Miocene. On the left side is a Smooth Hammerhead Shark (*Sphyrna cf. zygaena*), on the right is a Scoophead Shark (*Sphyrna cf. media*), the middle shark is a Sand Tiger Shark (*Carcharias taurus*), and they are chasing a school of fossil Manta rays (*Mobula loupiaensis*).

Cretoxyrhina mantelli was a large shark that lived about 100 to 82 million years ago, during the late Cretaceous period. It is nicknamed the Ginsu shark in reference to the Ginsu knife since it fed by slicing into its victims with its knife-sharp teeth. Over the past century, several preserved specimens have revealed a great deal of insight about the physical features and lifestyle of this ancient predatory shark. The fossil teeth of *C. mantelli* are up to 3 inches long and smooth-edged, with a thick enamel coating. *Cretoxyrhina mantelli* grew up to 30 ft long and exceeded the extant great white shark, *Carcharodon carcharias*, in size. *Cretoxyrhina* was the largest shark in its time and was among the chief predators of the seas. Fossil records revealed that it preyed on a variety of marine animals; mosasaurs *Tylosaurus*, plesiosaurs *Elasmosaurus*, bony fish *Xiphactinus* and turtles *Archelon*. This shark lived in seas worldwide, in the Western Interior Seaway of North America.

The Green River Formation is an extensive freshwater lake system. It started in the Late Paleocene, and ended in the Late Middle Eocene. It was in northeastern Utah, southwestern Wyoming, and northwest Colorado. This lake system had freshwater stingrays, *Heliobatis radians*, as well as a few undescribed rays. They ranged in size from 3 inches to 3 feet. It was first named by O.C. Marsh, in 1877. They had a maximum of three barbed spines, though usually found with two. How the rays first appeared in a land locked lake is a mystery. The large fish is a freshwater early paddlefish, *Crossopholis magnicaudatus*, the smaller ray is an undescribed genus, and the larger right one is *Heliobatis radians*.

A giant shark the size of a two-story building prowled the shallow seas 100 million years ago, new fossils reveal. The massive fish, *Leptostyrax macrorhiza*, would have been one of the largest predators of its day, and may push back scientists' estimates of when such gigantic predatory sharks evolved. About 100 million years ago Fort Worth, Texas was part of a shallow sea known as the Western Interior Seaway that split North America in two and spanned from the Gulf of Mexico to the Arctic. The vertebrae found there had stacks of lines called lamellae around the outside, suggesting the bones once belonged to a broad scientific classification of sharks called lamniformes that includes sand tiger sharks, great white sharks, goblin sharks and others. That vertebra came from a shark that was up to 32 feet long. As for the ancient shark's feeding habits, they might resemble those of modern great white sharks, who eat whatever fits in their mouth. If these ancient sea monsters were similar, they might have fed on large fish, baby pliosaurs, marine reptiles and even full-grown pliosaurs that they scavenged.

Edestus sp is a an eugenodontid holocephalia. It lived during the Late Carboniferous and has been found in North America and Europe. Its name means devour, Greek, edeste. It has long been considered to be an early shark, an eugenodontid, but recently it has been considered to be more similar to a chimerian, and is here depicted more like the latter than the former. It lived in marine deposits and one of the species, the appellee named *E. giganteus*, was nearly 9 meters long. It has been suggested to be similar to *Holicoprion*, because they share tooth whorls, however, in *Edestus*, the teeth were not in a circular tooth whorl, only a quarter of a whorl.

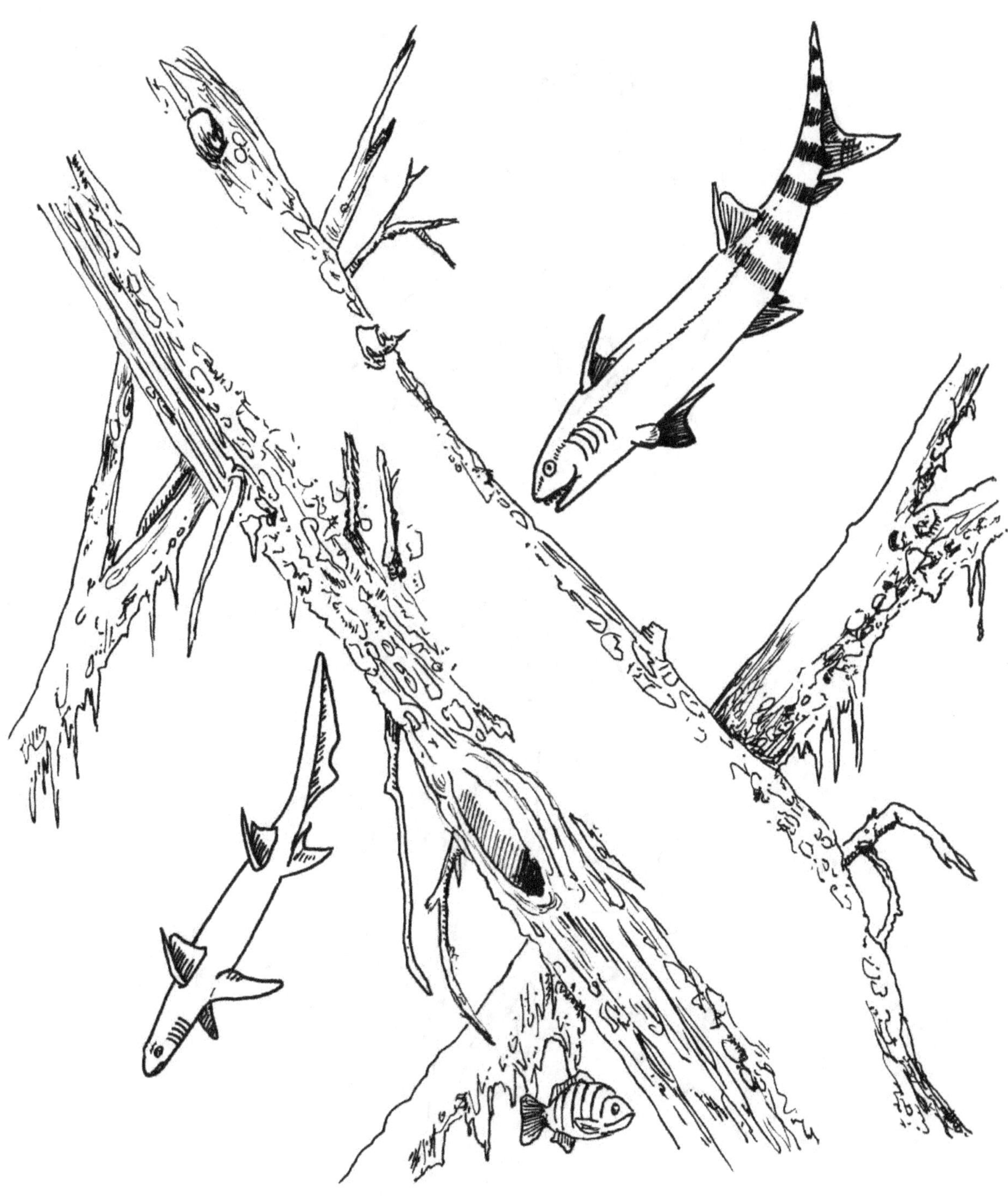

Prehistoric sharks were predators of other sea creatures, but many were prey themselves. Another fact is that many sharks ate other sharks. Here we see the larger shark *Sphenacanthus* chasing a *Tristychius*. *Tristychius* is an extinct genus of shark from the Carboniferous period. Fossils have been found in Scotland. *Tristychius* was a small shark, at about 2 ft long. It had a well-developed upturned caudal fin, similar to that of many modern sharks. Physically it may have resembled a modern dogfish. *Tristychius* also had spikes attached to the bases of its dorsal fins, probably for protection against predators.

Eonotidanus muensteri feasts on an ichthyosaur fall (similar to a modern whale fall) during the Solnohfen. The ichthyosaur is the long bodied short finned *Nannopterygius* sp. *Eonotidanus* is a member of the Sixgill/Green shark/Cow shark family (Hexanchdae). It was a small shark, about a meter long, while its modern relative grows to more than 28 feet. To the left is a *Phorcynis catulina*, and the right a *Hybodus fraasi*.

A fairly newly found shark ruled a warm lagoon 300 million years ago in what is now New Mexico. So far, the shark is dubbed "Godzilla shark" because of the shark's resemblance to the fictional Godzilla. It got its name for the following reasons: 1) the dorsal fin spines on the shark are huge relative to the rest of the body, like those seen on the back of Godzilla, 2) Like Godzilla, it has broad, short and sharp teeth, rather than long needle-like teeth seen in other sharks of that same time period, 3) the body was largely covered by coarse dermal denticles, giving it almost a reptilian feel when you look at the fossil (like the skin of a gila monster), and 4) compared to the rest of the fish and other creatures found at the locality, its huge. The average size fish here is just shy of being seven inches long. The largest shark fossil before the discovery of this new specimen was just shy of being a foot and a half long. Godzilla-shark was between seven to nine feet in length and would have terrorized the other relatively tiny critters of the area. Godzilla Shark was a ctenacanth. The shark's teeth seem to have evolved for a crunching grasp rather than a piercing grasp. It was probably more of a slower moving ambush predator, using quick burst of speed to capture fish and cruising close to the coast and in lagoons and river estuaries. Many thanks to artist and shark expert Ray Troll.

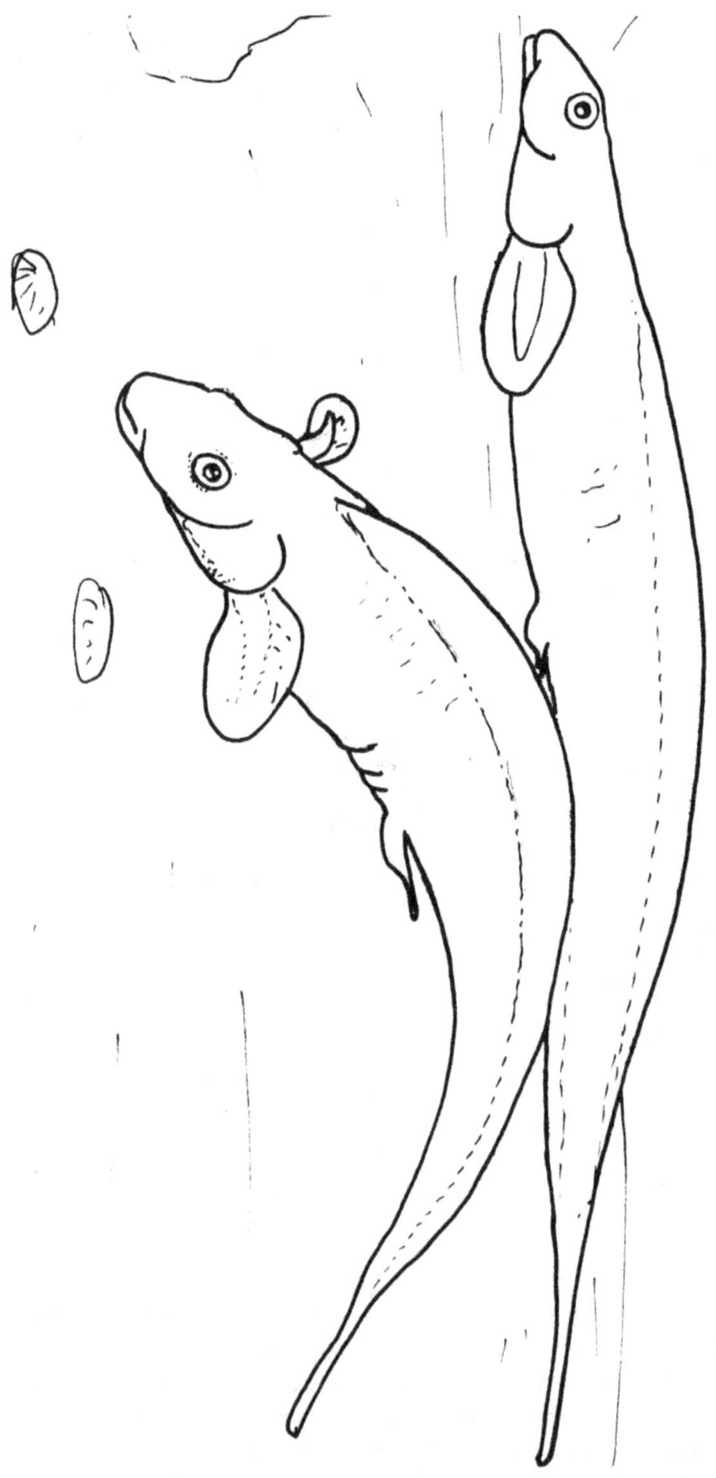

Chondrenchelys problematica was named by Traquair, in 1888. Its name means…because of its odd and troubling morphology. It has a long, eel like body, and is the earliest well preserved holocelophelian (chimeria). It comes from the Lower Carboniferous of Scotland, 336.5 mya, it was found in a near-shore environment, and was a bottom dwelling animal. It was about a meter long.

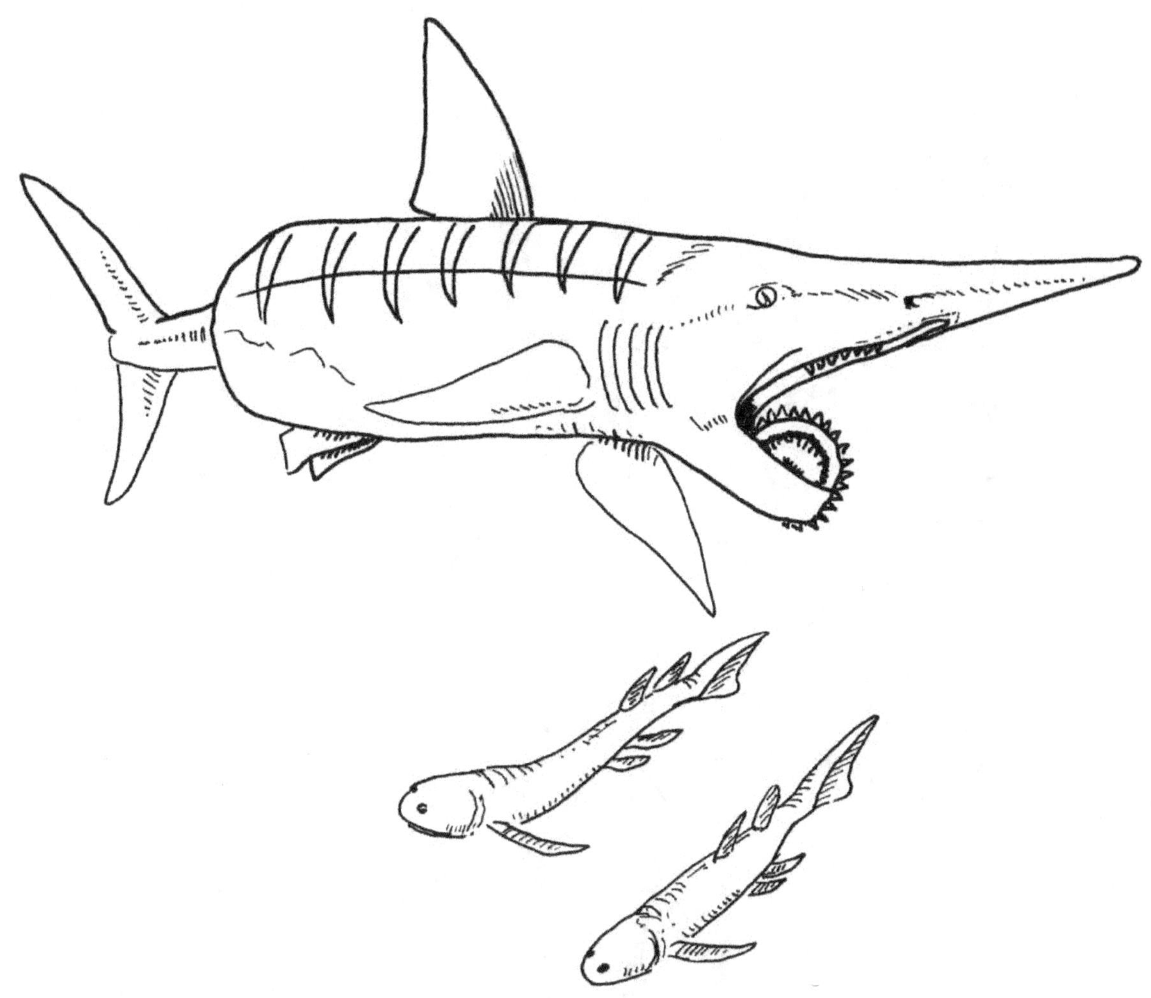

Sarcoprion (from the Ancient Greek for "flesh saw") is an extinct shark from the Permian of Greenland. Similar to other eugeneodontids such as *Edestus* and *Heliocoprion,* it was best known for its extremely bizarre tooth morphology compared to other species of sharks and their closest relatives, the chimaeras. Compared to other members of the Helicoprionidae, its "tooth whorls" were found to be sharper, more compact, and in better condition than other sharks of the time, and refrained from growing to extremely unwieldy forms that would raise questions about its ability to feed properly. The genus contains one species, *Sarcoprion* had a jaw and mouth structure which allowed it to be more hydrodynamic, reducing the size and shape of the tooth whorl and increasing the size of the rostrum. *Sarcoprion* is thought to have pursued smaller, fast-moving prey similar to today's mako shark. It had an average length of 20 ft from the two specimens discovered in Greenland. Using the compact tooth whorl during hunting, and any creatures that were wedged between its rostrum and its teeth were vertically thrashed to inflict maximum damage.

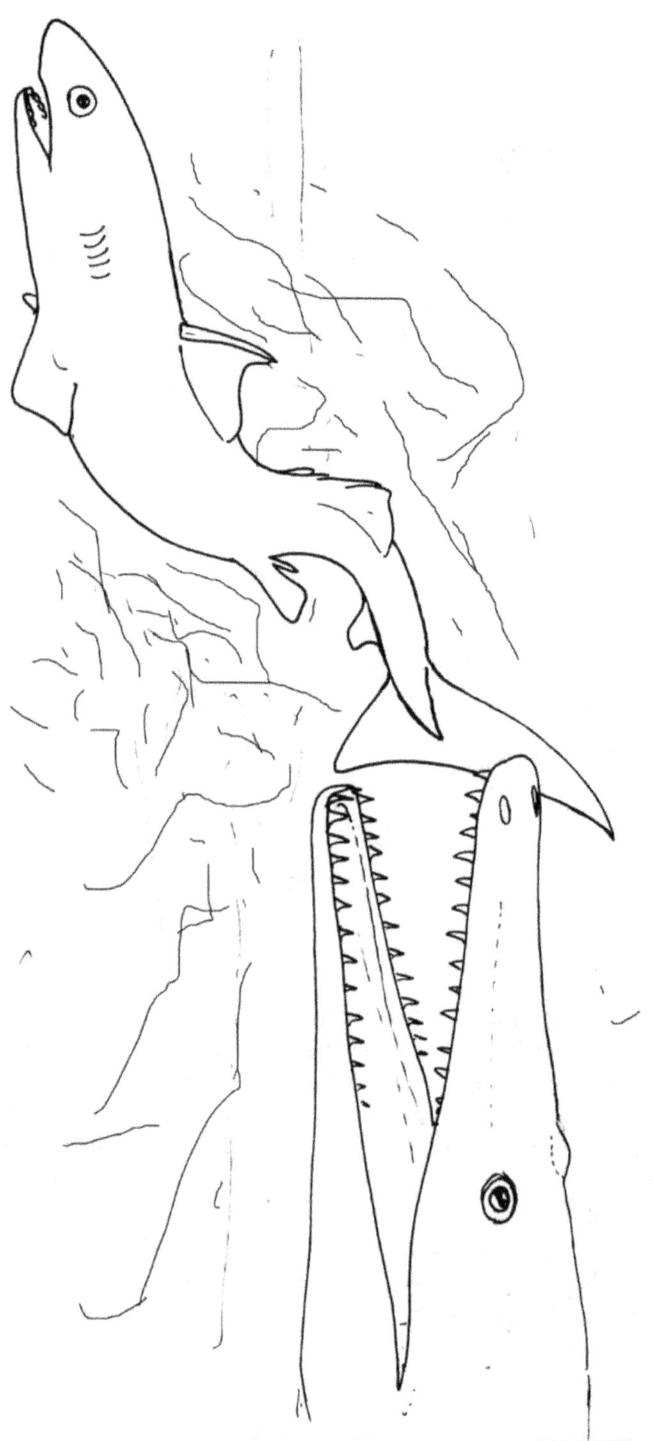

Wodnika striatula is a shark with an elongate body, short fins, and small tail. It is a small freshwater fish that is a meter long. It had a slender head with large eyes. The teeth were bean-shaped and slightly curved and must have fed primarily on hard-shelled animals like mussles, brachiopods and shellfish. Here an *Archegosaurus decheni* temnospondyl (early amphibian) chases a *Wodnika*.

Falcatus lived during the early Carboniferous Period in Bear Gulch bay in what is now Montana. It was about a foot long. It had prominent fin spines that curved forward over the head of the males, known due to the presence of valvae. The females did not have the spines.

Goodrichthys eskdalensis was described by Moy-Thomas, 1936. It was first found in Eskdale, Scotland, Lower Carboniferous, and it was about 2.5 meters. However, it has since also been found in North America, and a fragmentary braincase found in Texas, suggests it grew to nearly 7 meters! That is bigger than a great white shark. It is an early shark in the Ctenacanthoidea, family Ctenacanthidae. Their bodies are covered in compound dermal denticles (like really rough sand paper), with two dorsal fin spines and fins that are attached to the body. It was a marine shark, and was the biggest of its day.

Xenacanthus lived in the later Devonian period, and survived until the end of the Triassic, 202 million years ago. Fossils of various species have been found worldwide. This freshwater shark was about three feet in length. The dorsal fin was ribbonlike and ran the entire length of the back and round the tail. *Xenacanthus* may have swum very eel-like. A distinctive spine projected from the back of the head and gave the genus its name. The spike has even been speculated to have been poisonous, perhaps in a similar manner to a sting ray. This is quite plausible as the rays are close relatives to the sharks. The teeth had an unusual "V" shape. It probably fed on small crustaceans and heavily scaled fishes. As with all fossil sharks, *Xenacanthus* is mainly known from fossilized teeth and spines.

The hybodont shark, *Lonchidion* lived mainly in freshwater, though could go into marine waters. As a whole it had crushing teeth, though the teeth did have a ridge for cutting. It lived from the early Triassic to the Late Cretaceous. During the Early Cretaceous of Las Hoyas, Cuenca, Spain, two *Lonchidion's* swim the warm fresh waters, while the carchardontosaurid, *Concavenator* walks on the shore, and an *Europejara* fly's overhead. *Lonchidion* had been made a junior synonym of *Lissodus* for a few dozen years, but has now been shown to be a valid genus.

Squalicorax is a genus of extinct lamniform shark that lived during the Cretaceous period. The name *Squalicorax* is derived from the Latin meaning Raven Shark. There were many different species of *Squalicorax*. These sharks were of medium size; usually about 6 feet but could be twice that size in length. Their bodies were similar to modern gray sharks, but their teeth were like that of a tiger shark. Their numerous teeth were sharp and serrated (the only representative of the Mesozoic Lamniformes with serrated teeth). *Squalicorax* was a coastal predator, but also scavenged as evidenced by a *Squalicorax* tooth found embedded in the metatarsal (foot) bone of a terrestrial hadrosaurid dinosaur that most likely died on land and ended up in the water.

Tristychius arcuatus is a small freshwater shark that lived during the Lower Carboniferous of Scotland. It was about 60 centimeters long with a pointed snout, five gills, large pectoral and pelvic fins, and a short tail. The teeth are blunt, with one to three cusps. It belongs to the superfamily Hybodontoidea, family uncertain.

This deep sea-dwelling, serpentine "horror" is the frilled shark (*Chlamydoselachus*), one of the oldest living species on the planet. Its prehistoric contemporaries, such as the dinosaurs, died out long ago, but the frilled shark is still swimming around deep below the surface of the world's oceans. In its 80 million years on the planet, it has rarely come into contact with humans but a few have been caught and even filmed recently. At six feet long, the shark is named after its gills, which have frilly edges. Inside its short-snouted head are hundreds of oddly-shaped, needle-sharp teeth, neatly lined in 25 rows and perfect for latching onto prey.

Harpacanthus fimbriatus was originally described from the Lower Carboniferous of Scotland based on a single sharply curved spine armed with distal double row of elongate conical denticles/points. More complete specimens were found in Bear Gulch Limestone, Heath Formation, Montana, though other specimens have also been found in Illinois. It turns out the spines belonged on front of the head of Holocephalian, family Harpacantidae. The head had two paired spines on the head, which may be secondary sexual structures among the Holocephalimorpha. It had an elongate body, with a long dorsal fin, and was small, about 30 centimeters long. A *Harpacanthus* chases two polychaetae worms.

The horn shark (*Heterodontus*) is a species of bullhead shark, in the family Heterodontidae. It is endemic to the coastal waters off the western coast of North America, from California to the Gulf of California. The yard-long horn shark can be recognized by a short, blunt head with ridges over its eyes, two high dorsal fins with large spines, and a brown or gray coloration with many small dark spots. It has evolved very little from its prehistoric ancestors. Slow-moving, generally solitary predators, horn sharks hunt at night inside small home ranges and retreat to a favored shelter during the day. Adult sharks prey mainly on hard-shelled mollusks, echinoderms, and crustaceans, which they crush between powerful jaws and molar-like teeth, while also feeding opportunistically on a wide variety of other invertebrates and small bony fishes. Juveniles prefer softer-bodied prey such as polychaete worms and sea anemones. The shark extracts its prey from the substrate using suction and, if necessary, levering motions with its body. Horn sharks are harmless unless harassed. They are very old sharks that have survived prehistoric times changing very little.

One of the strangest looking Chondrichthyian are the Iniopterygians. The front fins are at the top of the scaleless body, and generally looked like modern chimaeroids. They are from the Pennsylvania age, Carboniferous period, of Ohio and Montana and they lived in the ocean. Though they look like flying fish, they were actually benthic feeders; the upper left is *Sibyrhynchus denisoni*, the middle and lower right is *Promexyele peyeri*, the upper right is *Iniopteryx rushlaui*, and the lower left is *Iniotera richardsoni*.

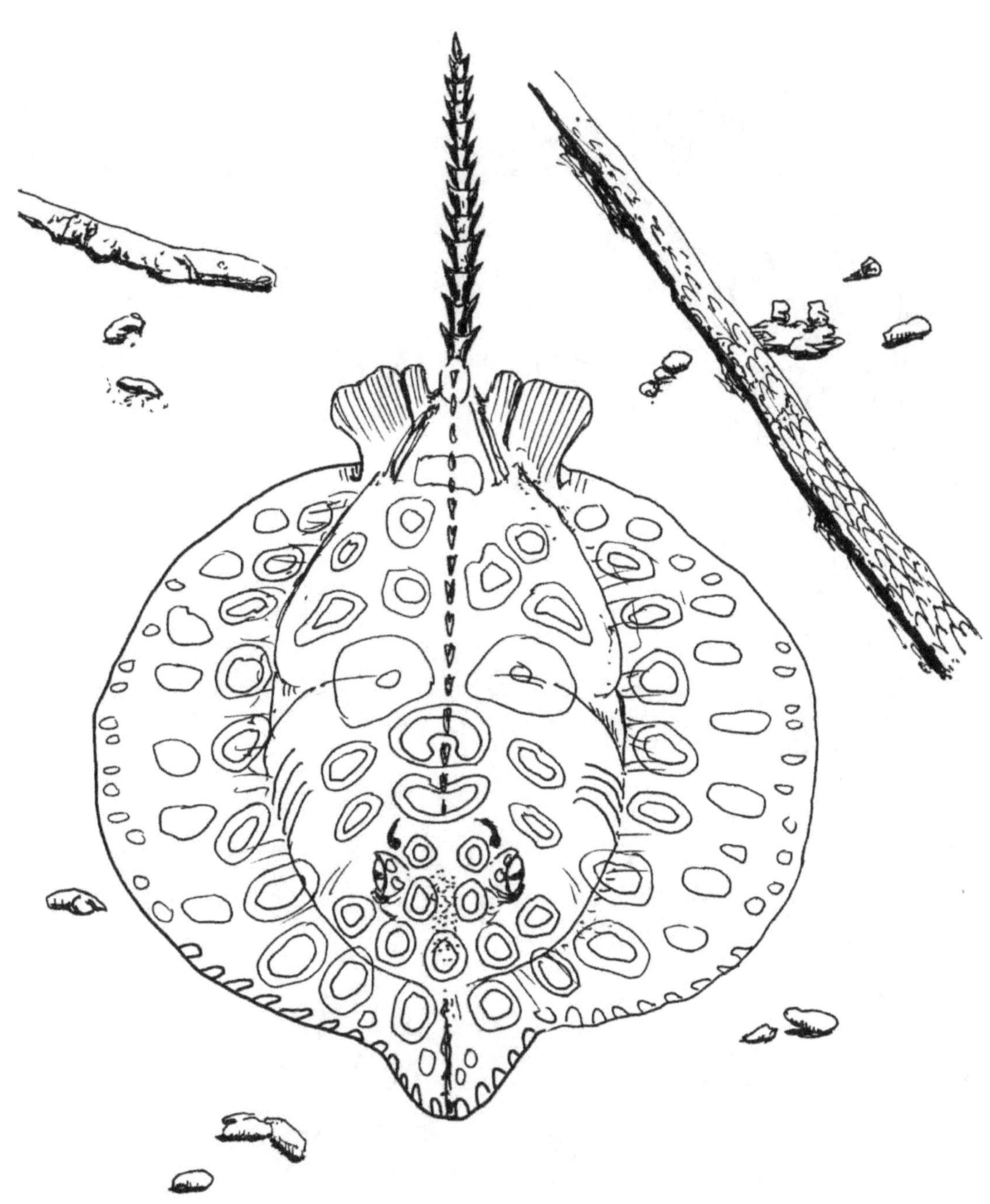

Cyclobatis is an extinct genus of stingray-like skate from the Upper Cretaceous of what is now Lebanon. The genus is typified by a circular form. The ray measures about 10cm or 20cm. In life the environment of this creature was a warm shallow sea. This fish had a very short tail, fitted with a venomous stinger.

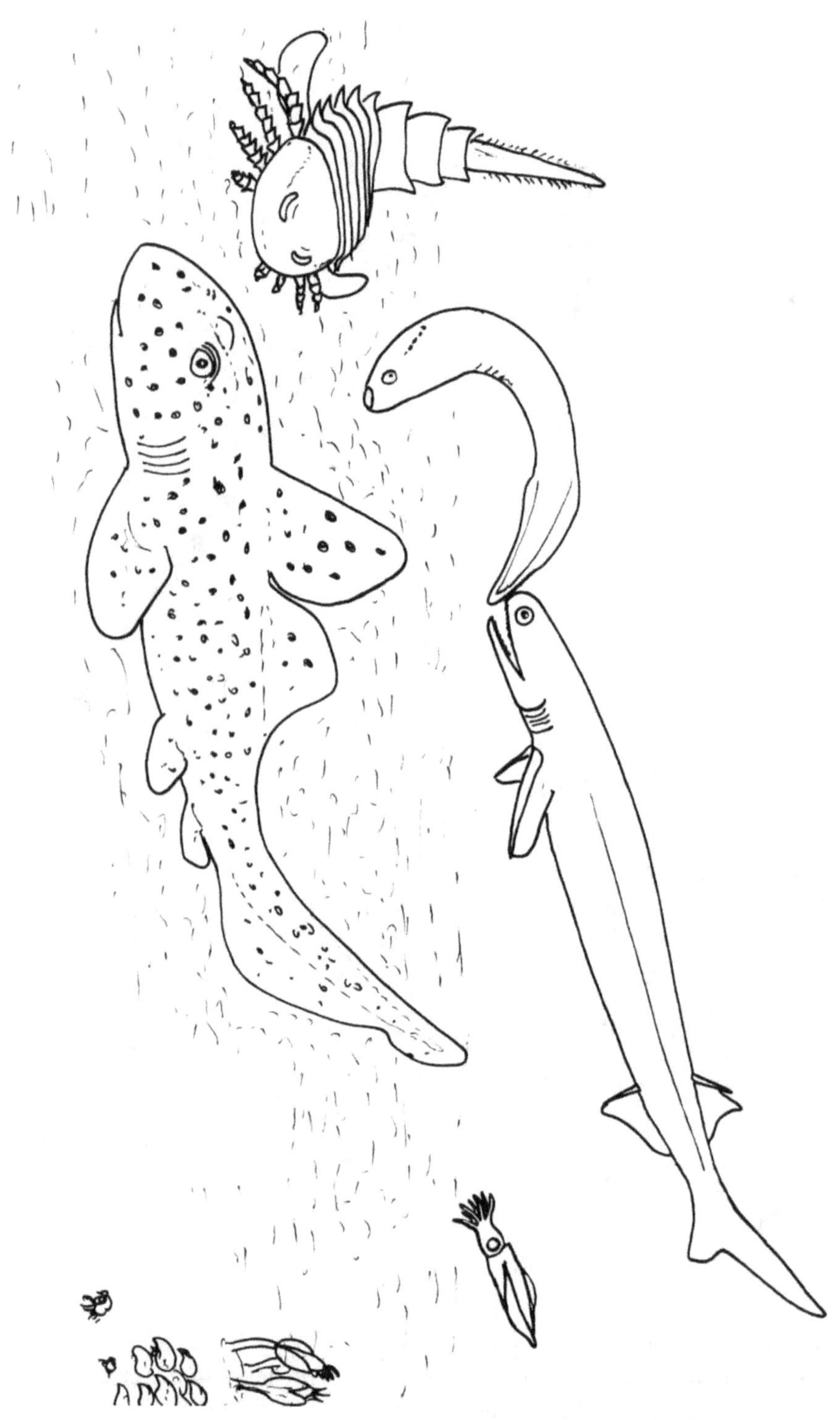

The Mazon Creek was part of the Francis Creek Shale member, Carbondale Formation, Middle Pennsylvania, Illinois. During that time period, the area was a lowland swamp that ran from the Appalachians west to the Middle North America. Numerous invertebrates and vertebrates have been discovered in the Mazon Creek. *Holmacanthus keithi* was described by Bardack, in Zangerl, 1997. It is a juvenile shark the preserved impressions of the skin fin, with poorly calcified skeleton. It was a bottom dwelling shark, and active predator. It was about 10 centimeters long, but it is unknown how big an adult would have gotten. The squid like cephalopod is *Jeletzkya douglassae*, The eurypterid *Adelopthalmus mazonensis*, an early lamprey *Gilpichthys greenei*, and *Acanththodes* swim around the shark.

Stethacanthus was another odd-looking genus of shark which lived from the Late Devonian to Early Carboniferous periods, dying out over 300 million years ago. Fossils have been found in Asia, Europe and North America. The name refers to the distinctive shaped first dorsal fin and spine displayed by mature males of the genus. *Stethacanthus* was around two feet long, and in many respects, had a shark-like appearance. However, it is best known for its unusually shaped dorsal fin, which resembled an anvil or ironing board. Small spikes (enlarged versions of the dermal denticles commonly covering shark skin) covered this crest, and the head as well. The crest may have played a role in mating rituals, aided in clamping to the belly of larger marine animals, or been used to frighten potential predators. This rat-fish shark may have been a slow swimmer and a bottom dweller.

Polysentor gorbairdi is a Subterbranchialia (near the inioterygians) from the early Pennsylvanian, Middle Carboniferous, Illinois. It was a small chondrichthyian with a large blunt head, long bodied, short fins, and lived in fresh water.

Ptychodus was a genus of extinct shell-crushing sharks from the Late Cretaceous. Fossils of *Ptychodus* teeth are plentiful in many of the Late Cretaceous marine sediments. There are many species among the *Ptychodus* that have been uncovered on all the continents around the globe. They died out approximately 85 million years ago in the Western Interior Sea, where a majority of them were found. The Genus name *Ptychodus* comes from the Greek words ptychos (fold/layer) and odon (tooth), so "fold teeth" describing the shape of their crushing and grinding teeth that were recovered in deposits. *Ptychodus* was about 30 feet long and had a massive arrangement of many, crushing plate teeth. It is believed that this Cretaceous macro-predator was the precursor to crushing plate teeth seen in many similar sharks and rays. *Ptychodus* was a predator that dined upon the extremely large bivalves and crustaceans inhabiting the Western Interior Seaway. One of the largest bivalves at the time was the 9-foot *Platyceramus*, a shelled mollusk that would have provided a difficult meal for any other creature, but with its crushing palate *Ptychodus* could have broken through this durable mollusk with ease. Giant ammonites, members of the Belemnite family, squid, and a variety of Cretaceous crustaceans would also make up the majority of the shark's food.

Cobelodus aculeatus belongs to the order Symmoriida, family Symmoriidae, and are among the best-known Paleozoic sharks. It lived during the late Pennsylvania (Upper Carboniferous) of Illinois. It had a short body, one dorsal vin, and two paired lower fins. Their skin is naked (i.e. lacks scales, scepter along parts of the lateral line). They are short bodied sharks, and about 200 centimeters (2 meters) long.

Megalodon (*Carcharocles megalodon*, also called *Carchodon megalodon*, *Otodus megalodon*), meaning "big tooth," is an extinct species of shark that lived approximately 23 to 2.6 million years ago, during the Early Miocene to the end of the Pliocene. There has been some debate regarding the taxonomy of megalodon: some researchers argued that it was of the family Lamnidae and closely related to the great white shark, while others argued that it belonged to the extinct family Otodontidae; presently, there is near unanimous consensus that the latter view is correct. Its genus placement, however, is still debated. Regarded as one of the largest and most powerful fish to have ever lived, fossil remains of megalodon suggest that this giant shark reached a length of 59 ft, though there are many other competing figures due to fragmentary remains. Their large jaws could exert an enormous bite force and their teeth were thick and robust, built for grabbing prey and breaking bone. Megalodon probably had a profound impact on the structure of marine communities. It probably targeted large prey, such as whales, seals, and giant turtles. Juveniles inhabited warm coastal waters where they would feed on fish and small whales. The animal faced competition from whale-eating cetaceans, such as Livyatan and ancient killer whales (*Orcinus citoniensis*), which likely contributed to its extinction. "Meg" as it is often called has attracted the imagination of many artists and authors. Illustrations and books about it abound.

Protospinax annectans is an enigmatic, rare shark from the Solnhofen of Bavaria, Germany. It had a flat body with large front fins. Ii looks like a cross between angle sharks and guitarfish. It was about a meter and a half long. It lived on the ocean floor and was probably not a free swimming shark. A long, eel like, unnamed shark swims near it. Above *Protospinax* is an ocean dwelling Metriorhynchid crocodile, with fins for legs, and a down turned tail like a shark. It lacked body armor.

Otodus was an extinct genus of mackerel shark which lived from the Paleocene to the Miocene epoch. The name *Otodus* comes from Greek for "ear-shaped tooth". This shark is mostly known from the fossil teeth which were large with a triangular crown, smooth cutting edges, and visible cusps on the roots. Some *Otodus* teeth also show signs of evolving serrations. Scientists suggest that this shark reached at least 30 ft in total length and maybe even 40 feet. *Otodus* had a worldwide distribution. *Otodus* likely preyed upon marine mammals, large bony fish, and other sharks. It was among the top predators of its time. Scientists believe that *Otodus* evolved into the genus *Carcharocles*, given substantial fossil evidence in the form of transitional teeth. These transitional fossils suggest a worldwide evolutionary event, and support the theory that *Otodus* eventually evolved into *Otodus aksuaticus* and initiated the *Carcharocles* lineage.

www.ingramcontent.com/pod-product-compliance
Lightning Source LLC
Chambersburg PA
CBHW081321250726
48662CB00008B/2689